AF599418

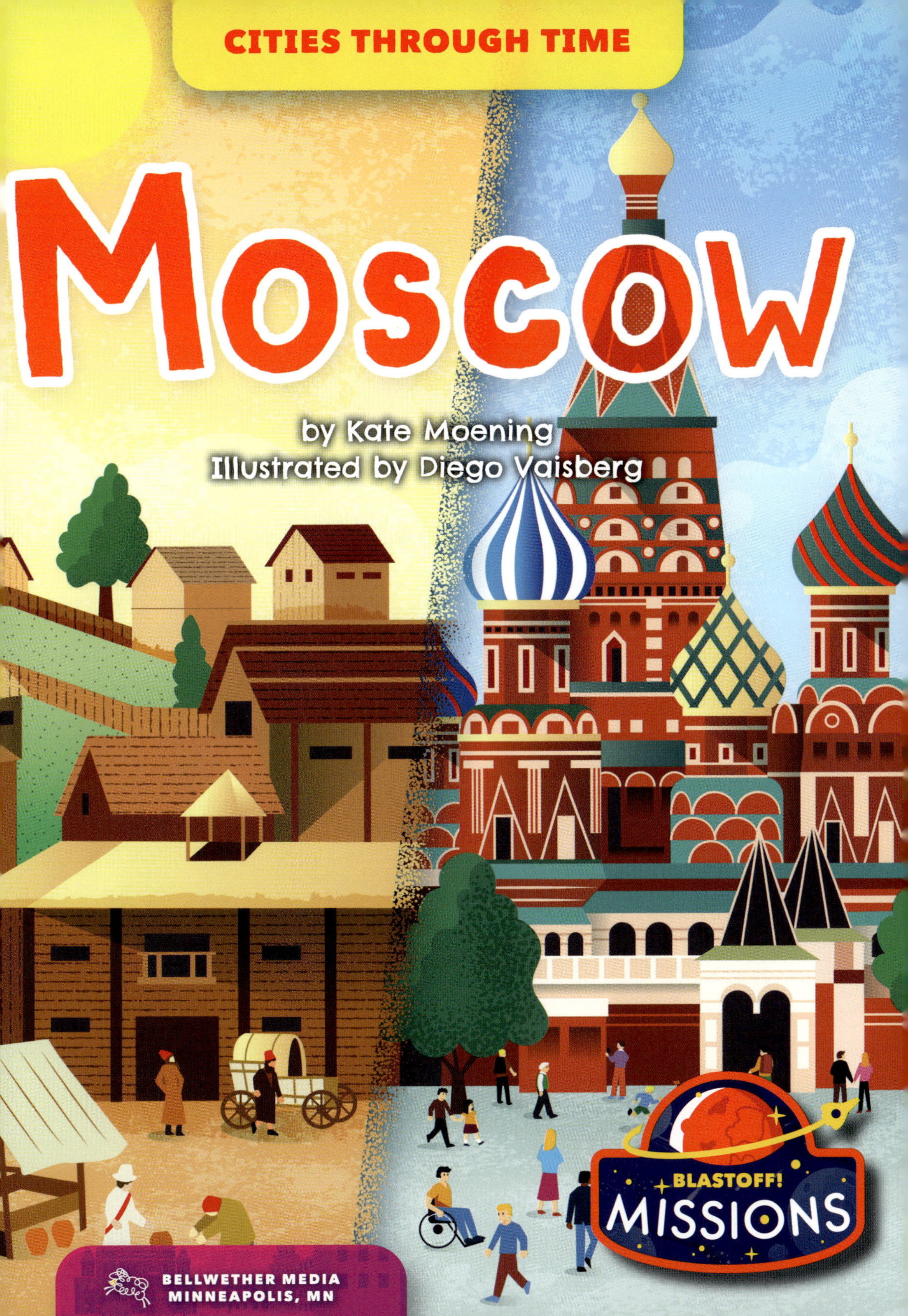
CITIES THROUGH TIME
MOSCOW
by Kate Moening
Illustrated by Diego Vaisberg
BLASTOFF!
MISSIONS
BELLWETHER MEDIA
MINNEAPOLIS, MN

Blastoff! Missions takes you on a learning adventure! Colorful illustrations and exciting narratives highlight cool facts about our world and beyond. Read the mission goals and follow the narrative to gain knowledge, build reading skills, and have fun!

Traditional Nonfiction

MISSIONS

Narrative Nonfiction

Blastoff! Universe

MISSION GOALS

- FIND YOUR SIGHT WORDS IN THE BOOK.
- LEARN ABOUT DIFFERENT PERIODS IN MOSCOW'S HISTORY.
- LEARN ABOUT LEADERS WHO HAVE SHAPED MOSCOW.

This edition first published in 2025 by Bellwether Media, Inc.

Library of Congress Cataloging-in-Publication Data

LC record for Moscow available at: https://lccn.loc.gov/2024046812

Editor: Christina Leaf Designer: Laura Sowers

Printed in the United States of America, North Mankato, MN.

Table of Contents

Welcome to Moscow!

Here we are in busy Moscow, Russia! Almost 13 million people live here.

People have lived here for hundreds of years. The city has seen **empires** and wars. Let's check out Moscow's past!

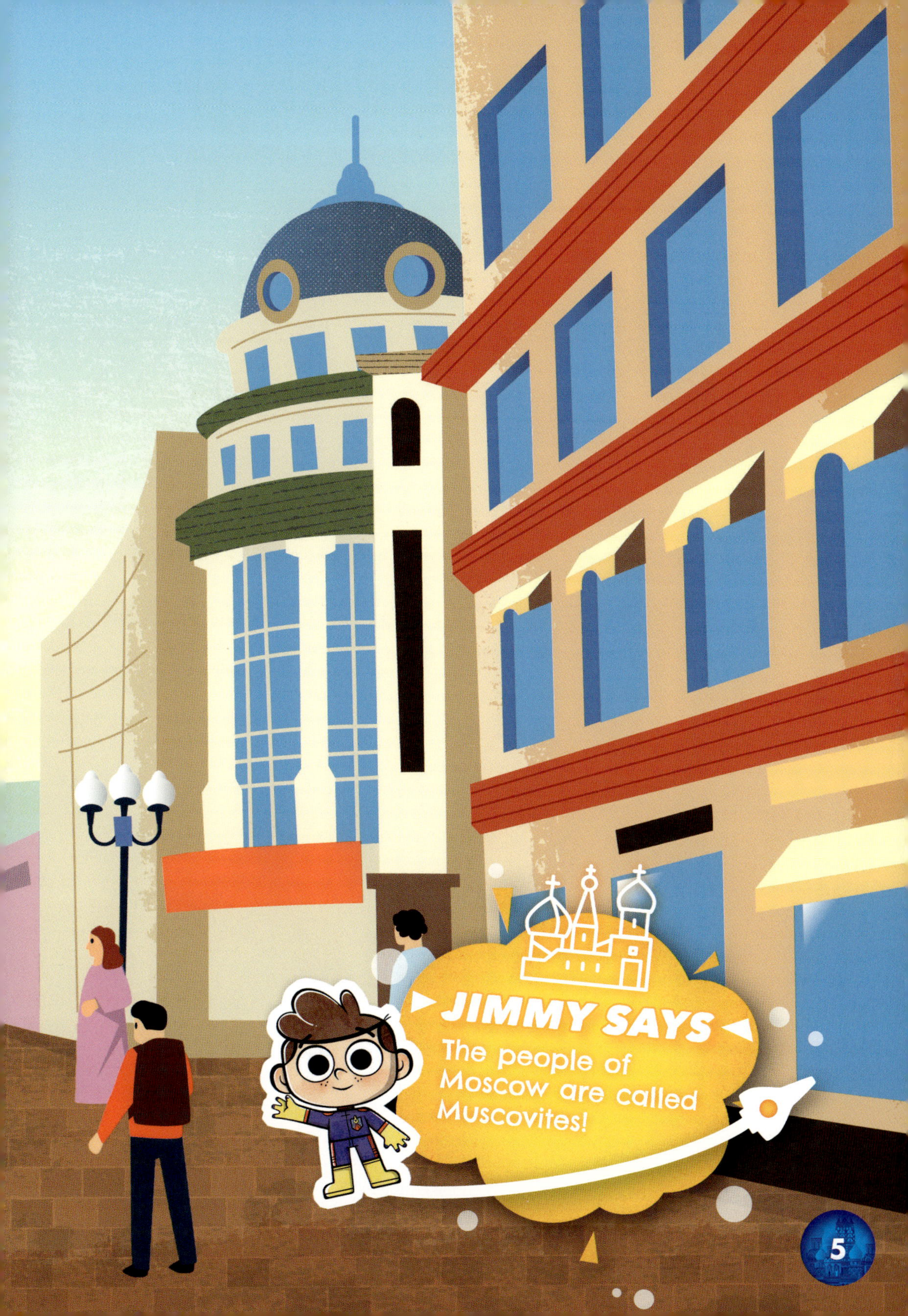
JIMMY SAYS
The people of Moscow are called Muscovites!

Moscow's Beginnings

1156

Prince Dolgoruky is building a huge **fort**! Workers use dirt and wood.

The fort sits high above the Moscow River. It will be called the Kremlin.

The Rule of Czars

1500s

Moscow is full of busy artists! Armor makers, **blacksmiths**, and weavers are hard at work.

Many sell their goods in Red Square. Traders come from many countries.

JIMMY SAYS
In Old Russian, the word for "red" also means "beautiful."
Red Square

Czar Peter I rules over Russia! In Moscow, people head to work in factories.

They will make clothes and sails for ships. Moscow is known for **textiles**.

1812

The French have **invaded** Moscow! Many Russians have already escaped. A huge fire breaks out. Many buildings burn.

The cold Russian winter is coming.
The French will be forced to leave.

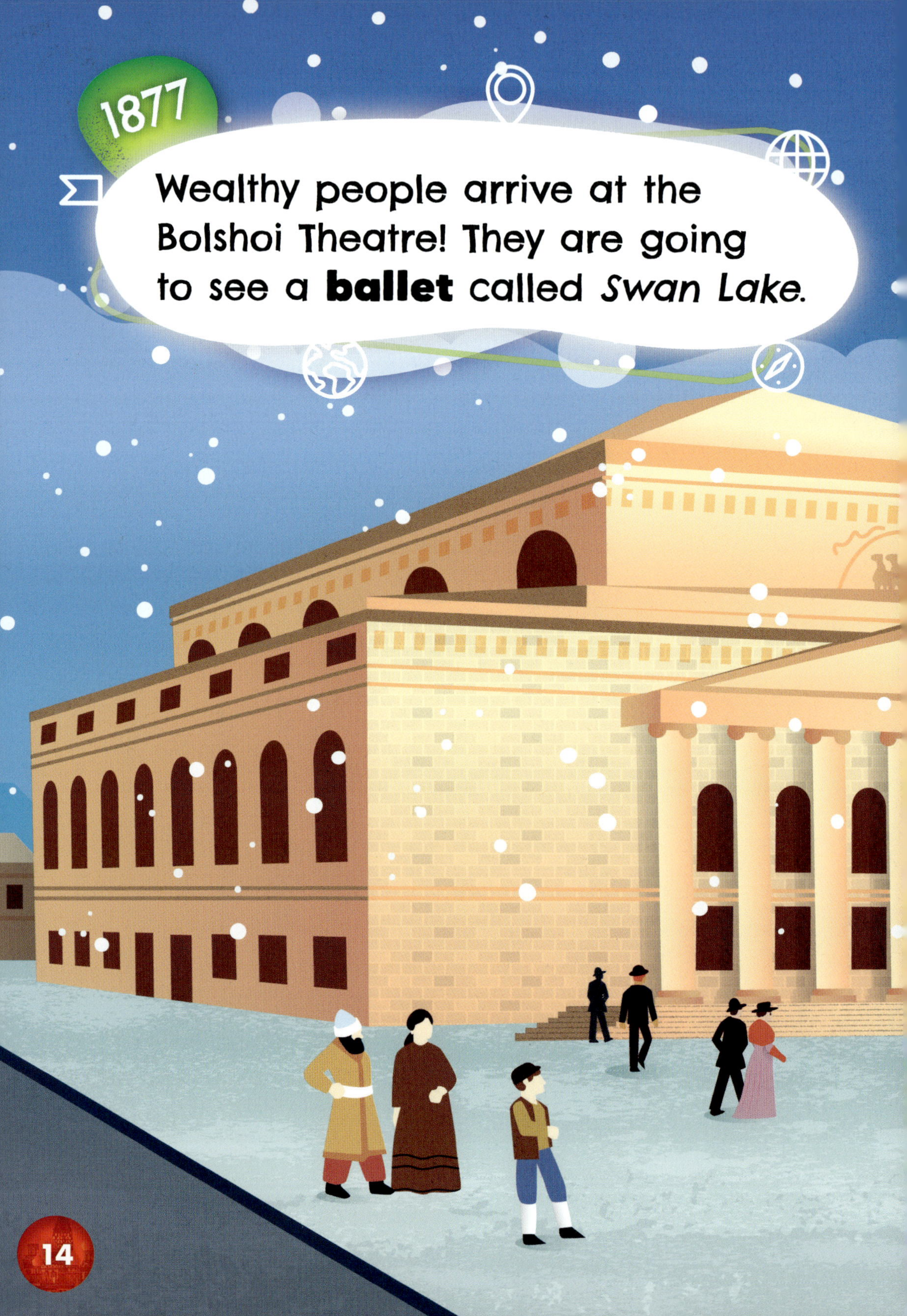
1877
Wealthy people arrive at the Bolshoi Theatre! They are going to see a **ballet** called *Swan Lake*.

Peasants watch them from the street. They have come to Moscow to find work.

A New Age

1922

The **Red Army** marches through Red Square. The march marks five years since the **Russian Revolution** began.

Soon leaders will form the **Soviet Union**.

1991
People try to take over
the Soviet Union's government.
Leader Boris Yeltsin stops
the takeover!

But the Soviet Union will break up soon. Many countries will form.
Boris Yeltsin

The City Today

Moscow buzzes with activity. People visit museums and parks. They watch soccer games.

Palaces, shops, and blocky towers line the streets. Past and present meet in Moscow!

Moscow Timeline

1156: Prince Dolgoruky begins building the Kremlin

1500s: Moscow is full of artisans, like armor makers and blacksmiths

early 1700s: Czar Peter I rules over Russia

1812: French troops try and fail to take over Moscow

1877: *Swan Lake* opens at the Bolshoi Theatre

1922: The Red Army marches through Red Square for the Russian Revolution's anniversary, and the Soviet Union forms

1991: Boris Yeltsin stops a takeover of the Soviet Union's government

Glossary

ballet—a kind of performance that uses dancing, music, and costumes to share a story or idea

blacksmiths—people who make or fix things made of iron

czar—someone who ruled Russia between the 1500s and 1917

empires—groups of countries or places that are controlled by one government

fort—a strong building used for protection

invaded—entered to take control through force

palaces—official homes of czars and other leaders

peasants—poor people who often worked on farms

Red Army—the army created after the Russian Revolution of 1917

Russian Revolution—an event in 1917 that removed Russia's czars from power and created a government of working-class people

Soviet Union—a country in eastern Europe and northern Asia from 1922 to 1991

textiles—fabrics that are woven or knit

To Learn More

AT THE LIBRARY

Hopkinson, Deborah. *Where is the Kremlin?* New York, N.Y.: Penguin Workshop, 2019.

The New York City Ballet. *Swan Lake*. New York, N.Y.: Little Simon, 2019.

Sabelko, Rebecca. *Russia*. Minneapolis, Minn.: Bellwether Media, 2023.

ON THE WEB

FACTSURFER

Factsurfer.com gives you a safe, fun way to find more information.

1. Go to www.factsurfer.com.
2. Enter "Moscow" into the search box and click 🔍.
3. Select your book cover to see a list of related content.

BEYOND THE MISSION

> WHAT FACT FROM THE BOOK DID YOU THINK WAS THE MOST INTERESTING?

> WHY DO YOU THINK MOSCOW HAS MANY DIFFERENT STYLES OF BUILDINGS? DRAW A PICTURE OF MOSCOW IN THE FUTURE.

> IMAGINE YOU MUST CREATE A BALLET FOR THE BOLSHOI THEATRE. WHAT WOULD IT BE ABOUT?

Index